Out Now!

Stella Parsons

Magazine Editor's Journal

On The Job Series 2
Out Now! — Magazine Editor
ISBN: 978-1-74164-287-2

Published by Blake Education Pty Ltd
ABN 50 074 266 023
Locked Bag 2022
Glebe NSW 2037

Ph (02) 8585 4085
Fax (02) 8585 4058

Email: info@blake.com.au
Website: www.blake.com.au

Written by Lisa Thompson
Publisher: Katy Pike
Editors: Paul O'Beirne, Eve Tonelli and
Emma Waterhouse
Designer: Cliff Watt
Printed by Tara TPS

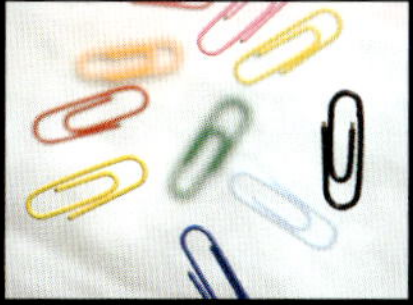

Contents

I'll organise lots of fun and games for the beach party.

Consumer magazines and trade magazines

Consumer magazines cover anything to do with fashion, gardening, entertainment, cooking, travel and cars. Trade magazines are more specialised, eg defence, aviation, **organic farming** and hotel management.

It's 8 am and I'm already in the office reading my emails — or at least the ones marked 'high priority', as there are so many. Our regular monthly issue has just gone to the printer, so we've turned our attention to the much-anticipated, bumper summer issue.

Mustn't forget!

Max West, one of the best young photographers around, has confirmed he will do a last-minute fashion shoot. That's a relief and very exciting!

The marketing department has asked for another meeting about the launch party for the summer issue. The theme for the issue is 'the best summer ever', so we're hoping to hold a night beach party. We like to throw a theme party with our yearly bumper issue. It is always eagerly awaited and provides great exposure for our magazine and our advertisers.

Max is very talented, so it's great to have him on board.

DYK? DIDYOUKNOW?

Oldest general interest magazine

The *Gentleman's Magazine* was first published in London in 1731. It was published for the well-educated public and had **articles** on politics and poetry.

BUMPER SUMMER ISSUE

HIVE MAGAZINE

Hive is a teen-**lifestyle** magazine. It covers everything from music, sports and health, to fashion and entertainment. It also includes special interest **features**, such as the article on skateboarding we're publishing in the summer issue. *Hive* aims to be at the cutting edge in content and style (ie, what we include in the magazine and how it looks). Our **freelance** artists, photographers, writers and stylists include some of the best young-adult talent you can find.

DYK? DIDYOUKNOW?

Hey, big spenders!

Australians are among the world's biggest magazine buyers. In 2006, there were an estimated 4 500 magazine titles available in Australia.

music

Our staff are like bees that travel to all corners of the globe to bring back the freshest, most contemporary and interesting images, stories and cool stuff to *Hive*!

My vision for *Hive* is that it should be like an exciting tour around our world — a peek into what's happening for teens everywhere. All our staff love what they do, and I think that comes across in the quality of *Hive*. The readers seem to love it too!

entertainment

We're big on teamwork at Hive.

Mags beat TV

Studies show that, dollar for dollar, magazines are more effective than television at generating brand awareness and product sales. Magazine advertisements can target the audience they want by appearing in specific magazines.

Skateboarding is so in right now.

I'm thinking of ways to incorporate a beach hut into our beach party — it could serve as a changing room.

As I read through the articles for the summer issue, I notice there's an interesting one on making skateboards and another on secret beach huts that kids have built. Both are great for the summer issue.

There's a huge buzz around the summer issue — and this one is shaping up to be our biggest ever. Our readers and advertisers look forward to it as we always try to do something to make these issues different and collectable. We have a few surprises in the pipeline — which is a good sign.

Putting together this issue can take eight months to plan and organise. This is fairly stressful as we still have to publish the monthly issues of *Hive* in the meantime.

I make changes and add comments to the articles. Then at 10 am, the meetings start. As Editor-in-Chief, my job involves approving every article, picture, **layout**, headline and cover line. I have meetings scheduled with most of the departments — features, art, advertising and marketing. I also have phone meetings with some of our freelance photographers, stylists and writers. Something tells me today is going to be a whirlwind of problem-solving and decision-making.

Cover lines

Cover lines are the small lines of text that appear on a magazine cover to advertise and explain what can be found inside.

Joke: what's the difference between a magazine editor and an artist?
Answer: the spelling.

Meeting with the marketing department — our main aim is to keep our readers happy. If we achieve that, our sales will be good.

Great article, just needs some small changes — see margin notes.

Email | Files | System | Applications | Help

Inbox 42

Reply

Send

Sent

Seen

From Stella
To Sally
Subject What a day!

Hi Sally,
Here's my chaotic schedule!

Lunchtime — Match photos with files; confirm and style fashions; approve layouts; chase up writers and photographers.

2 pm — Do interview at local radio station to promote our new competition — one lucky reader will win a trainee job with us!

3 pm — Meet with the marketers about the launch party.

4 pm — Back in office to jot down new ideas for future issues; check layouts for the summer issue.

Radio interviews can be quite daunting, but they are a great way of marketing *Hive*.

Sally, one of the **editorial** assistants, is kept busy all day chasing up various people.

I spend quite a bit of time in taxis!

Top three

The top three subject categories for magazines are —

1 entertainment/celebrities
2 fashion/accessories
3 food/nutrition.

Reading about what we eat is popular.

Blogger: ME

At 6 pm, some skateboarding pictures from a photo shoot come in. They look fantastic! This summer issue is certainly taking shape. I'm excited as I leave the office, with a few more feature articles to read at home and a couple of layouts to mull over before the morning.

open skateboard pics

Joke: Why did everybody in the marketing department have wet hair?
Answer: Because they were brainstorming.

DYK? DIDYOUKNOW?

Mag mad

In Australia, 71 percent of men and 81 percent of women regularly read at least one consumer magazine — that's nearly 13 million Australians!

How I became a magazine editor

Growing up, I never really thought about a career in publishing — but there were always lots of magazines at home, and I read every one about fashion and music. Mum liked the celebrity news; Dad was into science and gardening magazines. My two older brothers subscribed to magazines on surfing, music and motorbikes.

I used to do a lot of daydreaming while flicking through those magazines. For me, they have always been about **escapism** and making my world a little bigger.

I enjoyed writing too, and when I was 14, I won a writing competition run by a magazine. Even then I never imagined I'd end up running one!

Joke: Why are celebrities so cool?
Answer: Because they have so many fans.

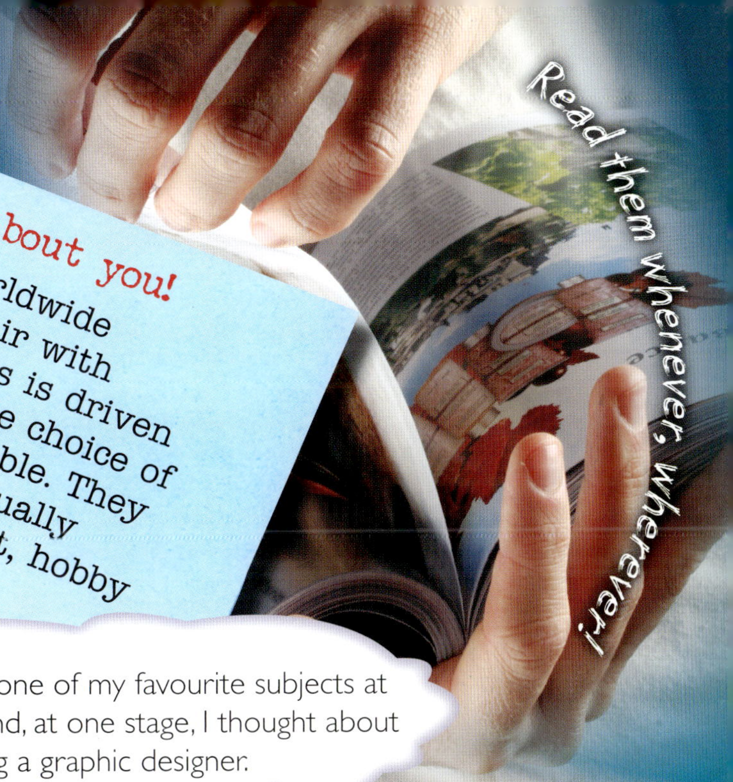

Read them whenever, wherever!

Mag about you!

The worldwide love affair with magazines is driven by the wide choice of titles available. They cater to virtually every interest, hobby and activity.

Art was one of my favourite subjects at school and, at one stage, I thought about becoming a graphic designer.

one of our previous cover girls

Cover girl

The term 'cover girl' first appeared in English in 1915. A cover girl is a female whose photograph features on the front cover of a magazine. Models, celebrities or entertainers frequently appear on magazine covers. The aim is to increase the readers' interest — and sales!

Where to next?!

Table no.2, your order is ready!

I was very snap happy!

On finishing school, I studied journalism at university, where my interest in photography grew. After university, I went travelling. I funded my trip by waitressing, but I constantly sent photos and articles into magazines and local papers to try to get published.

Eventually, I landed a job writing entertainment and restaurant **reviews** for a weekly, newspaper magazine. I was flying off in all directions, interviewing people and eating yummy food! I did that job for about three years.

I gained a world of experience by travelling and learned lots about food when I was waitressing — that really helped later when I had to write restaurant reviews. At an industry function, I met Kieran Walsh, the publisher of *Hive*. He loves adventure and **adrenalin sports**. I've always admired the exciting style of his magazine. It pushes the boundaries both in look and content. It's not a predictable magazine delivering the same thing every issue.

Hive likes to inspire, surprise and amaze its readers. Kieran and I clicked. We shared similar ideas about magazines. It was really inspiring!

One day, as I was about to hop on a plane to New Zealand, I got a call from Kieran offering me a job as the new Editor-in-Chief at *Hive*. It was a dream come true — and it came out of the blue! I was nervous and excited by the challenge.

That call was two and a half years ago, and I am still nervous and excited about the challenge of doing every *Hive* issue — particularly the summer issue and this one looks like it will be our biggest one yet.

I got lots of experience interviewing and writing reviews.

I'll never forget that call at the airport!

Kieran's love of adventure shines through Hive's style and content.

AN EDITOR-IN

An Editor-in-Chief is responsible for a magazine's look and content. They are a business manager and journalist rolled into one. They need strong skills in research and communication, and need to have a love of publishing.

Business skills

- solid understanding of the publishing process
- understand my readers and what they want
- knowledge of business management
- leadership skills
- communication and people skills

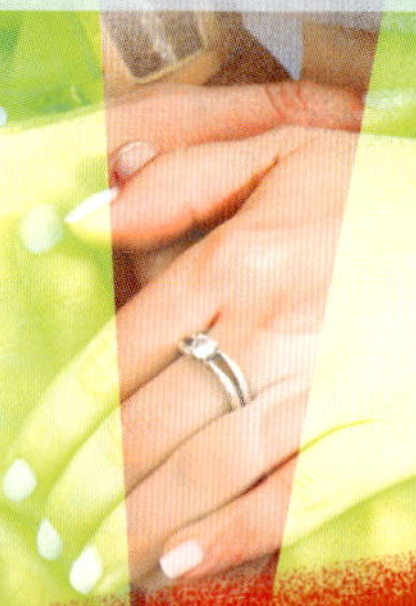

A STRONG TEAM SPRIT IS ESSENTIAL AT WORK — THINGS GET DONE WITH LESS FUSS AND THE PLACE RUNS SMOOTHLY.

Wearing the business manager's hat

An Editor-in-Chief, like me, needs to understand their market and work out how to keep existing readers as well as attract new ones. I manage budgets, work on marketing **campaigns** and bring in new advertisers.

BE PASSIONATE ABOUT YOUR FIELD — WHETHER IT'S SPORT, NEWS, ENTERTAINMENT . . .

CHIEF'S JOB

Wearing the journalist's hat

I also lead and manage the editorial team, so I need to have a strong vision for the type of articles that appear in the magazine. This is called an editorial **strategy**. I must also have a basic understanding of media law.

Journalist skills

- **analytical** abilities
- evaluating (assessing) the quality of written work
- writing skills
- editing skills
- knowledge of media law

BUDGETING IS A REAL CHALLENGE.

YOU DEFINITELY NEED A GOOD BUSINESS HEAD TO BE A MAGAZINE EDITOR — A BIG PART OF THE JOB INVOLVES BUSINESS MANAGEMENT.

THE BUCK STOPS WITH THE EDITOR-IN-CHIEF

Tough decisions

The Editor-in-Chief makes tough decisions. This means taking credit when things go well, but also taking blame when they don't.

An article that proves to be **controversial** can be a major headache for the Editor-in-Chief. They must carefully consider the consequences before authorising any article for print. For example, printing something **defamatory** about someone.

The ten qualities of successful editors

1. curiosity
2. **empathy** with readers
3. self-confidence — the ability to follow your instincts
4. fearlessness — especially when dealing with advertisers, publishers and the finance department!
5. **stamina** — both physical and mental
6. ability to encourage sensational performances from your staff
7. strong editorial skills
8. the ability to surround yourself with people more knowledgeable and talented than you
9. being able to say 'no' when something is not up to standard
10. strong **mentor** and leadership skills

A TALENTED TEAM IS WORTH ITS WEIGHT IN GOLD!

TV, RADIO, CINEMA AND EVEN NEWSPAPERS CANNO MATCH MAGAZINES FOR THEIR INTIMATE RELATIONSHIP WITH THEIR READERS.

Mags are best

Advertisers love magazines. They provide advertisers with choice — from the huge audience of the most popular women's titles to tiny, **niche** audiences of specialist trade magazines. The ability of magazines to target their audiences, and the ease with which consumers can choose a magazine to suit their needs, makes them perfect for advertising.

Who runs a magazine?

CONGRATULATE STAFF ON A JOB WELL DONE, BUT KNOW WHEN TO ASK FOR MORE.

As Editor-in-Chief I report to the Publisher. She manages all aspects of the publishing business, including contracts, finance, sales, marketing and production.

The Managing Editor works for the Chief, and manages the in-house and freelance feature writers.

The Creative Director is responsible for the overall look of the publication. They oversee the **branding** of the magazine and ensure the image of the magazine matches the Editor-in-Chief's vision.

WHO'S WHO AT HIVE MAGAZINE?

The size of a magazine's team depends on the amount of work to be done — the more issues, and the larger they are, the more people are needed to do the work. *Hive* is a thick magazine that comes out every month, so we have many staff.

Our magazine is broken up into departments. As Editor-in-Chief, it is my job to oversee all departments and roles to ensure the creation of an exciting publication and a healthy business.

The finance department, like the rest of us, likes to see rising profits.

Features department

This department includes a senior writer who writes special-interest pieces for each issue. There's also a features editor who works with freelancers on specific articles.

Fashion, health and beauty department

The fashion, health and beauty editor oversees the content. The senior writer writes and sources information for this section. There's also an editor's assistant who assists the editor and writer.

the features writers start their morning

Maggie, our fashion spy, keeps her eyes peeled for the latest trends.

Lifestyle department

The lifestyle editor is in charge here. This department includes a sports writer, a music and entertainment writer, and the gadget and technology writer. They also have an assistant editor to help them out.

A sports writer in the field!

Art department

The art department works with the Editor-in-Chief, Creative Director and the production department to come up with the look of each issue. The department includes the Art Director, a senior designer and other designers.

The creative Director stimulates creative ideas.

Photo department

This department works with the Creative Director and the Art Director sourcing photos and pictures for each issue. A photo editor, photo researcher and photo research assistant are also employed here.

photo editing

printing presses at work

Production department

The production department works with printers and distribution companies to make sure the magazine is produced and delivered on time. It includes a Production Director and Production Manager who ensure the smooth running of the department.

Advertising department

The advertising department finds new advertisers and works to keep existing ones. It includes an advertising director, an advertising manager and an advertising coordinator. The amount of advertising sold for each issue often determines the size of each issue. This department really is a hive of activity!

Freelance contributors

Our pool of talented freelancers sets *Hive* apart from other magazines. Freelancers are creative people who contribute on an issue-by-issue basis, depending on the look and content of a particular issue. Each issue, *Hive* uses different photographers, writers and illustrators, stylists and designers.

Marketing and promotions department

The marketing and promotions department works on increasing the **profile** of the magazine. It also works with the advertising department on special-event promotions and competitions. It includes a marketing and promotions director, a marketing and promotions manager and a marketing and promotions coordinator.

Freelancers can be expensive, but it's worth it as they're fexible and hardworking.

Marketing is full of innovative people who love coming up with new ideas.

Max Lambin
Dept: Lifestyle

As assistant to the lifestyle editors, I'm responsible for managing the flow of people in and out of the office. I also read and edit our readers' letters (some get published), so I get to see what our readers are really thinking — that's very valuable information.

I especially like getting positive feedback from readers — it makes my day.

Wendy Bell
Dept: Photo

As a photo editor, on any given day I might meet with photographers, plan shoots, scout locations, arrange travel plans or sort through piles of invoices and messages! Planning a photo shoot is hard because if something can go wrong, it will! Once it rained for a whole week on a tropical island beach shoot, so we had to do the whole thing indoors!

I love my job. I've never been bored!

Big business

In 2005, about US$385 billion was spent on advertising worldwide. This may increase to US$500 billion by 2010.

READERS AND RESEARCH

Who is the average *Hive* reader?

Magazine editors must know and understand their readers. This allows them to decide what kind of stories to publish, and the look of the magazine. Connecting with readers is one of the key factors to increasing sales and producing a successful magazine.

Hive reader profile

Age: 13-19
Gender: male and female

The *Hive* reader is …

- sporty
- fashion-oriented
- optimistic
- a real individual
- tech savvy
- media aware
- curious
- motivated
- a music lover
- creative

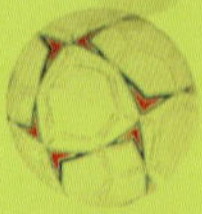

Know your audience

Magazines, like other businesses, undertake market research to find out what their customers want. This can be done by conducting surveys, test marketing (asking a test group what they think) or even simply encouraging reader feedback.

DYK? DIDYOUKNOW?

Super-subscribe me

Subscribing to magazines is usually cheaper than buying each issue in a newsagency (since you get a discount for paying in advance). You also have the convenience of having them delivered to your home. You need never miss out on your favourite magazine again!

COOLHUNTING

Coolhunting is a modern method of market research — literally hunting down what is 'cool'. For fashion labels, magazines and music makers, it's important to know what young people think is the latest, cool thing. So they hire coolhunters to research and even carry out undercover cool investigations!

PROGRESS MEETINGS FOR THE BEST EVER SUMMER ISSUE

One of our freelancers has taken fantastic photos to go with this story.

MUSIC FESTIVALS ROCK!

Meeting with the writers

We're including some of our readers' favourite summer memories in the biggest article in the summer issue. It's looking good and reads easily. I think it'll work well for general interest, and of course will delight the readers who contributed!

Our senior features writer, Amy, has almost finished her article on summer sports. She'll have no problem meeting the deadline.

We also go through the film and gadget reviews.

At the end of the meeting we decide to add another article about summer music festivals. This issue is going to really appeal to our readers as it's so varied — and as the saying goes, 'variety is the spice of life'!

Meeting with the art department

We go over the layouts. They are taking shape. Some of the advertisers have prepared special ads just for this issue and they look fantastic.

WHAT DID THE WRITER SAY TO THE EDITOR? PROOFREAD CAREFULLY TO SEE IF I ANY WORDS OUT.

The layout artists will let the Managing Editor know if the articles need cutting to fit the layout. This is called copyfitting.

A DESIGNER CHECKS THE LAYOUT BEFORE HANDING IT OVER FOR OUR APPROVAL.

We decide to change some of the **FONTS** used in the layouts. Even though they look good, they are too hard to read.

Meeting with art and production departments

We decided to use gold and silver metallic type on the cover. We chose the cover photo early, because it was striking and simple. The test runs are back from the printer and the gold type doesn't look like we imagined so we'll go with the bronze instead. We also decide to run with a mini-version of this artwork for the launch party tickets.

MY FAVOURITE STORY WAS ABOUT TWO KIDS LEARNING TO SNORKEL WHILE ON HOLIDAY IN GREECE.

On location at the 'Fun in the Sun' photo shoot

We are down the coast at a wonderful beach called Dolphin Bay. The photographer, Max West, the models and crew arrived last night — before the shoot — and stayed at a nearby hotel. It's an early start and they have to be on location before sunrise.

* * * * *

It's still dark outside. The models are getting their hair and make-up done. Because it's a beach theme, the look is natural, but a little make-up and hair styling is still needed. (The models in photo shoots are never natural! They are always styled and **manipulated** to get the required 'look'.)

Max and his assistant visited the location yesterday to get ideas for the kinds of shots they want. The theme is "golden summer days", so the look is to be dreamy, as though you are remembering the greatest summer day ever.

This guy's got the golden, summer day vibe we're after!

Max is a perfectionist, so he will take hundreds of photos and pick the best from them.

Photo editing

Photo editing is changing photos to make them more appealing than the originals. This is common practice in magazine publishing, especially with shots of models. Photo editing makes models look younger, slimmer, smoother and more tanned than in real life. Some people believe this causes self-esteem problems for teenagers, who want to look like people they see in magazines. It is impossible for them to do so because the photos themselves are not real!

A make-up artist styling one of the models before the shoot.

DYK? DIDYOUKNOW?

Freebies

A new **phenomenon** is happening in the magazine industry (in Europe, particularly). Magazines are being given away free! This may seem like madness, but it's a strategy that's proving to be effective. The advertising income that the publisher receives easily covers the costs of production and, in fact, increases profits. This practice is especially popular in Spain.

On Location

Max begins taking photographs just as the sun is rising. He takes lots of photos of the beach setting. I know they will be absolutely fantastic.

the shoot begins

Just as he's taking some photos of surfers, we see them — the famous dolphins of Dolphin Bay! We are all very excited and it gives the day a really special feel. Max excitedly takes photos of them — perhaps we can use some in our summer issue.

Max's assistant takes some shots too.

DYK? DIDYOUKNOW?

In the beginning …

Fashion photography was first used in French magazines in the early 1900s. The New York-based *Vogue* magazine also contributed to the beginnings of fashion photography. Their rival, *Harper's Bazaar*, became another leader in using fashion photography and the two companies were groundbreaking in the field throughout the 1920s and 1930s.

Example of an 1800–1900s magazine, Retro styles can still be in fashion now.

The stylist is putting the finishing touches to the jewellery that is laid out on shells for close-up photographs. It's important to get all the shots we've planned for, so I constantly refer back to the schedule to check we're on track.

one of our jewellery shots

1 pm — we're supposed to be breaking for lunch but Max decides he wants the models to pose with some of the locals.

6 pm — the sun goes down. The final shots of the series are taken of the beach bonfire with all the crew around.

11 pm — back at the hotel we look through the day's work. The photos look awesome. It really does look like the dream summer's day that it was!

The models and locals had a great laugh posing for photos!

Looks just right!

Stylists work with photographers to organise and arrange shots so that they convey exactly the look and feel that the advertiser wants.

Styling can take hours!

Looking back – the first magazines

The word 'magazine' was first commonly used in 1731 with the publication of *The Gentleman's Magazine* by Edward Cave. Its aim was to entertain with stories of crime and romance. It was very popular, not just sold but also rented in hotels, coffee and barber shops. Soon after, *The Lady's Magazine* was published.

Early magazines did not restrict themselves to leisure interests but often had political and religious content. In the mid-1700s, magazines did not always have what we now see as covers. Many had their cover page as a table of contents, or they began an article on the cover. The first teen magazines appeared in America and England in the 1940s.

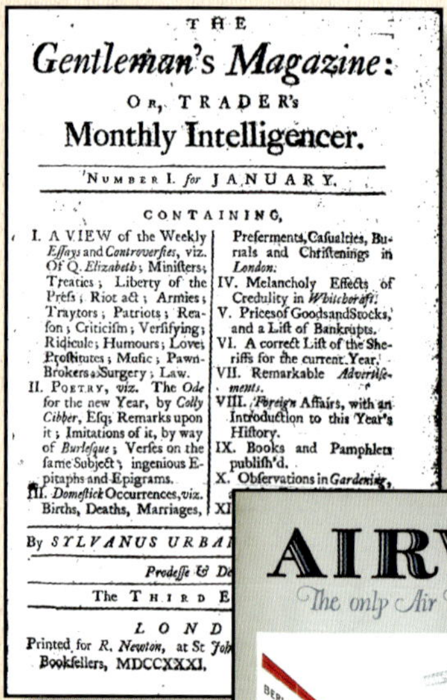

THE
Gentleman's Magazine:
Or, TRADER's
Monthly Intelligencer.

Number I. for JANUARY.

CONTAINING,

I. A VIEW of the Weekly Essays and Controversies, viz. Of Q. Elizabeth; Ministers; Treaties; Liberty of the Press; Riot act; Armies; Traytors; Patriots; Reason; Criticism; Versifying; Ridicule; Humours; Love; Prostitutes; Music; Pawn-Brokers; Surgery; Law.
II. Poetry, viz. The Ode for the new Year, by Colly Cibber, Esq; Remarks upon it; Imitations of it, by way of Burlesque; Verses on the same Subject; ingenious Epitaphs and Epigrams.
III. Domestick Occurrences, viz. Births, Deaths, Marriages,
Preferments, Casualties, Burials and Christenings in London.
IV. Melancholy Effects of Credulity in Witchcraft.
V. Prices of Goods and Stocks, and a List of Bankrupts.
VI. A correct List of the Sheriffs for the current Year.
VII. Remarkable Advertisements.
VIII. Foreign Affairs, with an Introduction to this Year's History.
IX. Books and Pamphlets publish'd.
X. Observations in Gardening, ...

By SYLVANUS URBAN ...

Prodesse & De...

The Third E...

LOND...

Printed for R. Newton, at St Joh...
Booksellers, MDCCXXXI.

Illustrations from magazines published in the early 1800s

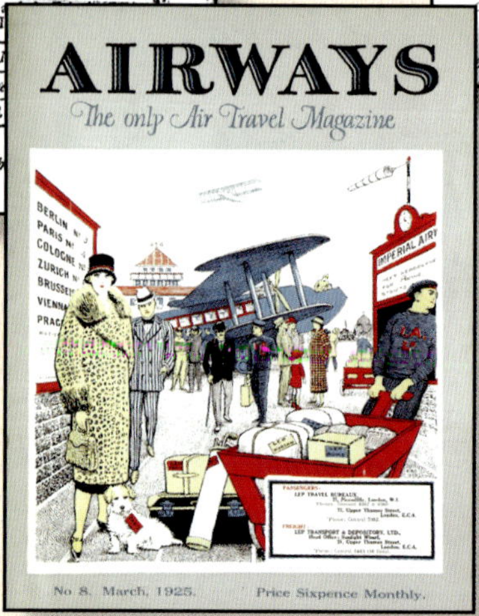

a 1925 travel magazine

an English science magazine from 1839

Magazines galore and more!

There's now a magazine for practically every imaginable interest, from fashion or food, to football or fishing.

There are more magazines today than ever before. Magazines both inform and entertain. It's this magical combination that has kept sales rising for nearly 300 years.

Advertising plays a key role. Depending on the market, advertising brings in about half of a magazine's revenue.

Advertising different products, eg makeup, lowers magazine costs.

How many writers does it take to change a light bulb?
Two. One to change the bulb and one to tell a long story about it.

Ad/edit ratio

For most weekly consumer magazines, the ratio of advertising pages to editorial pages is generally 45–50 percent advertising to 50–55 percent editorial.

Why we love magazines

Magazines are popular because people like the experience of reading them and flicking through the pages. They make them feel more informed. People also see magazine reading as time to relax and a way to have some time out for themselves. We don't need any special technology for magazine reading. We can do it anytime, anywhere, as long as we have light!

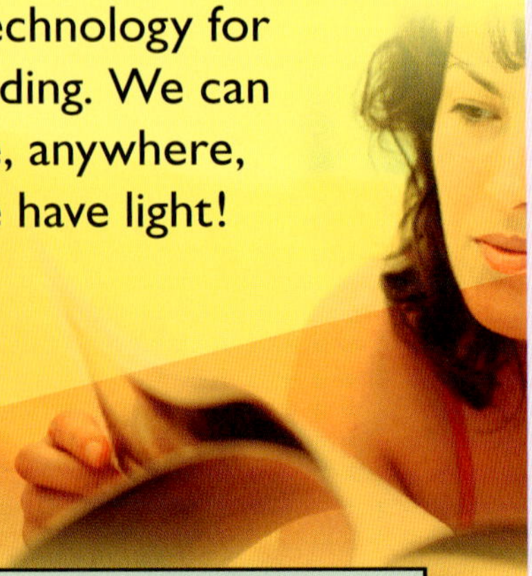

Time out

Comments

"It's quiet time."

"It's an escape."

"It's important for me to feel comfortable when I read."

"Reading this magazine is a bit of luxury."

"The magazine takes my mind off other things that are going on."

"Reading a magazine is my time alone."

DYK? DID YOU KNOW?

THE MOST EXPENSIVE MAG!

Wilmott is a finance magazine containing cutting-edge research, new products, book and software reviews, and in-depth analyses of financial markets. You can buy six issues a year for a mere $390. That's $65 each!

That's a lot of money!

It makes me smarter

comments

"It keeps me up to date on things that are important to me."

"I get ideas from the magazine."

"It addresses issues or topics that are of concern to me."

"The magazine gets me thinking about things."

WWW

Market research shows that magazine readers are likely to go to the World Wide Web to research topics they read about in magazines. They're also more likely to save magazine pages with Web addresses for future reference. In a recent Canadian study, 57 percent of magazine readers said magazines influence how they get information from the Internet. These findings are good news, especially for advertisers.

The Internet brings the world to us.

WHY ADVERTISERS LOVE MAGAZINES

The magazine experience

Reading a magazine is a relaxing and engaging experience. Statistics show an average reader spends around 45 minutes reading each issue.

Advertisers love magazines because it lets them engage with a consumer — they have the reader's full attention. Research shows that most people are more focused when reading a magazine than when watching the television or listening to the radio.

When ads come on the radio, my mind immediately wanders.

Top three advertising categories for teen magazines

1. fashion
2. entertainment/technology
3. food

Advertisers hope that focused attention generates more sales for their products.

Why advertisers choose magazines

She seems focused on her magazine — which means bigger sales for the advertisers inside!

❶ People are more focused when reading than when watching television, so they are more likely to remember the ads.
❷ Advertisers can target their market directly. The consumer of the magazine is their consumer as well.
❸ Positive consumer experiences with magazines boost the impact of magazine advertising.
❹ People often read magazines multiple times, and share them with other people, giving the advertisers added exposure.
❺ Magazine ad content makes people laugh, cry, think, desire, ponder, smile and more. In short, magazine ads make people react and connect with brands.

Making mags attractive

Many newspapers include free magazines, particularly on weekends. These may be monthly magazines or weekly inserts. Advertising covers the cost to the publisher, while the reader is more tempted to buy the paper because it comes with a free magazine.

Newspapers dangle free magazines in front of customers to encourage them to buy.

Another marketing tool is the 'free gift', eg a bag, lipstick or book. The occasional 'freebie' lures readers, especially those who may not be regular customers, to buy the magazine.

THE BUMPER ISSUE TAKES SHAPE

THE BIG DAY GETS CLOSER: LOOKS LIKE I STILL HAVE SOME WORK TO DO.

EIGHT DAYS TO GO

Now it's only just over a week until the printer's deadline.

Layouts have come in from the art department. They are checked and rechecked. There needs to be font changes to some of the photograph captions, but otherwise they're looking good.

We discover that some advertisers have not provided final artwork for their ads yet. The advertising department gets busy hunting down the missing artwork. Meanwhile, a couple of articles are still missing pictures, so the photo guys chase up the photographers.

I do a read-through to make sure all the headings and captions read well. I mark up last-minute changes and corrections.

EVERYTHING GETS CHECKED AND RECHECKED

DAN GETS ON THE PHONE TO FIND THE MISSING PICTURES.

JUST A FEW, TINY CHANGES

Proofs of the cover with the revised colours are back for approval. It looks just as I had imagined it. That earlier decision to switch to bronze has paid off.

Five Days to Go

I meet with the marketing department for an update on the progress of the launch issue beach party. I scan the RSVP list. Most of our big advertisers are coming, as well as many of our freelancers — great!

Marketing gives me a schedule for the radio and TV interviews. They have me lined up to do heaps of promotion the day the magazine comes out.

THERE'S GOING TO BE A HUGE PARTY WHEN THIS IS ALL FINISHED!

3 PM

Now, the all-important meeting with MY bosses — the owners of the magazine. They want to hear directly from me how the magazine is doing. I've prepared a full presentation, and armed with all my statistics and notes, I feel confident in telling them that we'll produce the best summer issue ever.

CAN'T FORGET ABOUT THIS MEETING!

WHERE ARE THOSE PHOTOS?

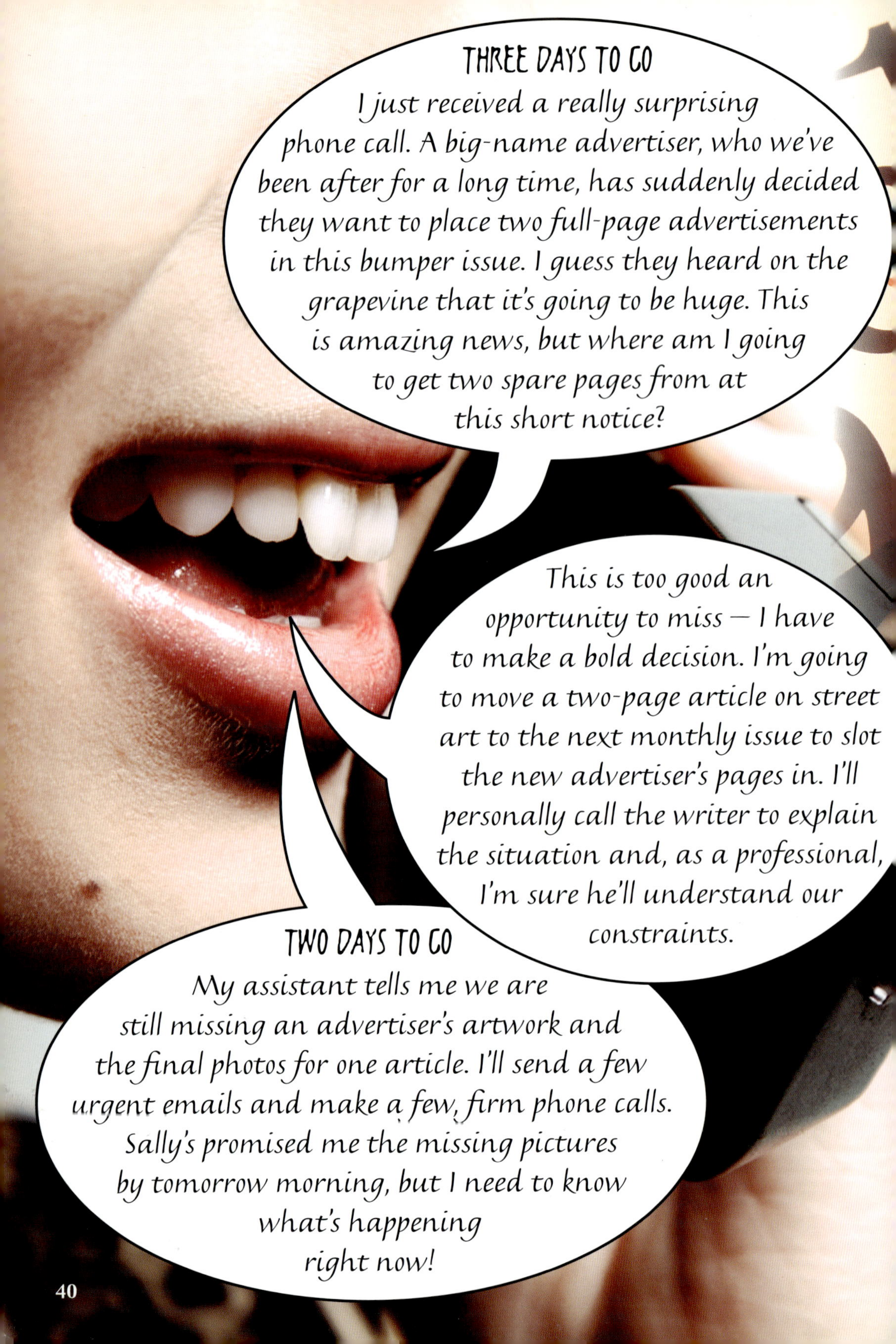
THREE DAYS TO GO
I just received a really surprising phone call. A big-name advertiser, who we've been after for a long time, has suddenly decided they want to place two full-page advertisements in this bumper issue. I guess they heard on the grapevine that it's going to be huge. This is amazing news, but where am I going to get two spare pages from at this short notice?
This is too good an opportunity to miss – I have to make a bold decision. I'm going to move a two-page article on street art to the next monthly issue to slot the new advertiser's pages in. I'll personally call the writer to explain the situation and, as a professional, I'm sure he'll understand our constraints.
TWO DAYS TO GO
My assistant tells me we are still missing an advertiser's artwork and the final photos for one article. I'll send a few urgent emails and make a few, firm phone calls. Sally's promised me the missing pictures by tomorrow morning, but I need to know what's happening right now!

ONE DAY TO GO!
Long hours for the art department and one final read-through for me. It feels like I've read the magazine 100 times, but I need to make sure everything is just right.
Why was the photographer in such a hurry? Because he knew it would be all over in a flash.
OK, phew! Those missing images turned up. Everything has been approved, so I'm going to give the final go-ahead to the printer. No matter how organised we are, it always seems like a mad rush for the last few days!
The printer has finally started!

Here it is!

The bumper summer issue of *Hive* is in! Everyone grabs a copy and flicks through it madly.

I am so relieved the cover looks fantastic! I walk down the street and see it in the newsagencies. Is it me or does that awesome metallic cover catch the eye brilliantly? I watch as two people grab copies, have a flick through, and then buy our magazine!

All the work was worth it. It really is the biggest and best bumper summer issue ever!

I race back to the office to begin my radio interviews, and then it's a quick sprint to the television station to appear on the afternoon kids' program *The Shed*. It's go, go, go …

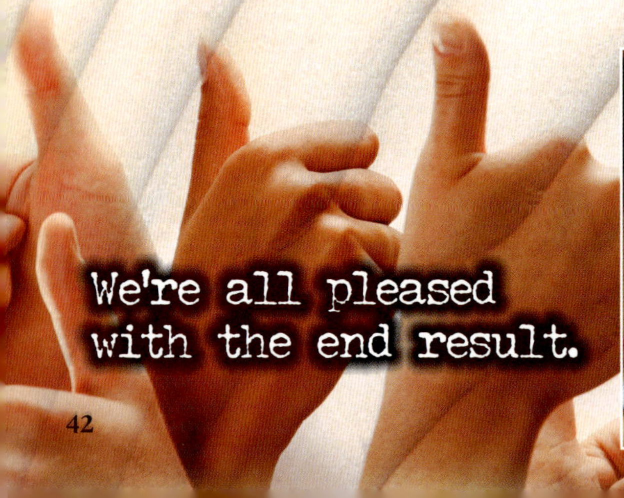

The launch party

Susan from Marketing gets ready for the beach party!

Great bonfire!

The beach bonfire is lit as the sun sets. We all want to celebrate the success of this issue, and *Hive* in general. Our sales are up and we have also attracted more big-name advertisers. *Hive* just gets bigger and bigger, which is great news for us and our advertisers.

I give a thankyou speech to all the people who have contributed and congratulate everyone on their hard work. It's a fun night for everyone, and Mandy and Dan, from the photo department, get some great shots, so we can share some of the fun in our next issue.

The Hive team relax on the beach, and the party goes on well into the night.

Thankfully, tomorrow is the weekend and I get to sleep in. But on Monday, I will be in the office to begin the next issue. The buzz at *Hive* magazine never stops, and be warned … it's addictive!

FOLLOW THESE STEPS TO BECOME A

magazine editor

1 Volunteer for the school paper to build your writing and editing skills. Finish school with the best grades you can get, especially in English and art.

Getting into papers or magazines early is a good idea!

2 Apply to local newspapers or magazines for an evening or summer apprenticeship while you are still at school. It may be unpaid, but the experience will be invaluable.

3 Study for a tertiary qualification in journalism or communications. Tertiary and private colleges provide diplomas in these fields. You could also apply to university to do a degree course.

4 Employers place great emphasis on work experience, so no matter which course you do, keep writing. Research magazines so you understand the style of articles they publish. You then have a better chance of them publishing articles you submit.

education + experience = success!

How do you get straight As? By using a ruler.

It's going to take a lot of drafts!

Red-hot fact!

Since employers value work experience so highly, people generally work their way up from a junior writer to a features editor, and then perhaps finally to an Editor-in-Chief position.

Doing professional apprenticeships once you've finished full-time study can be a huge plus as editors will often hire people they already know.

You may have to work long hours — especially when deadlines loom — and writers may require careful handling. But seeing the finished product that you have helped create is amazingly satisfying.

You'll need to work up to being in the big chair.

Now, where did I put that phone message?

opportunities for magazine editors

There are many related careers for editors, including —

- other forms of publishing, eg books, commercial
- digital and online publications, eg websites, e-books
- recruitment agencies — as someone who employs other editors
- newspapers
- copywriting
- freelance journalism.

Glossary

adrenalin sports — adventurous sports that make your heart beat faster
analytical — using logical reasoning to understand something
articles — pieces of writing in newspapers or magazines
branding — overall style and impression of something; the image of a consumer product or service, usually controlled by a marketing department
campaigns — planned series of actions to achieve a result
consumer — person who buys products or services
controversial — something that causes a lot of discussion or argument
defamatory — something that attacks a person's character or reputation
editorial — article which expresses the editor's or publication's opinion
empathy — understanding how another person feels
escapism — thinking pleasant or fantasy thoughts instead of thinking about real life; daydreaming
features — special articles in a magazine that are intended to stand out
freelance — someone who works for themselves and sells their work to more than one employer

layout — way something is visually arranged
lifestyle — way of living that reflects a person's values, attitudes and what is important to them, eg sporting lifestyle etc.
manipulated — changed or controlled something to make it what you wanted
mentor — to wisely advise someone junior or less skilled than yourself
niche — specific area suited to a particular person or group
organic farming — farming without using chemicals
phenomenon — something that happens, especially in a remarkable way
profile — short description of someone's character or life
reviews — newspaper or magazine article that gives an opinion on a product or service, eg a book or film
stamina — energy to do something for a long time
strategy — clever scheme or plan to achieve a goal
subscribe — to receive something, like a magazine, on a regular basis by paying in advance for a certain period

Index

other titles in the series

Pit Stop
Auto Mechanic

Toon Talent
Animator

Under Construction
Builder

What's Cooking?
Chef

Listen Up!
Sports Trainer

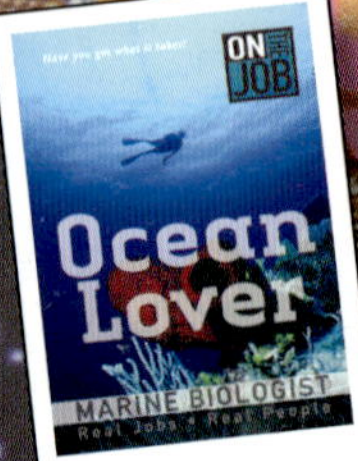

Ocean Lover
Marine Biologist

Style File
Fashion Designer

Animal Antics
Zoo Keeper

Let's Party
Event Planner

Emergency! Emergency!
Firefighter

1, 2, 3, 4
Choreographer

Child's Play
Early Childhood

Courtside
Lawyer

Trauma Alert
Emergency Nurse

Working the Land
Farmer

Eyes for Evidence
Forensic Scientist

Game On!
Games Developer

Ready for Take-off
Pilot

Lights, Camera, Action!
TV Producer